T0095350

Saved from Suicide
by
The Lord's Prayer

A Memoir of My Extraordinary Encounters with Our Source

Oliver H. Jobson

WESTBOW°
P R E S S
A DIVISION OF THOMAS NELSON
& ZONDERVAN

Copyright © 2015 Oliver H. Jobson.
www.oliverjobson.com

Final editing - Karol Jobson - kcjobson@gmail.com
Associated editor - Alex S.
Page design - Peter Stephenson - peter.fineprint@gmail.com
Associated designer - Alysha Smagorinsky
Portrait - Linda Constant Photography - www.lindaconstant.com
Cover - Igor Gottschalk, architect/graphic artist (London/Cologne) -
www.igorgottschalk.com

All rights reserved. No part of this book may be used or reproduced by
any means, graphic, electronic, or mechanical, including photocopying,
recording, taping or by any information storage retrieval system
without the written permission of the publisher except in the case
of brief quotations embodied in critical articles and reviews.

WestBow Press books may be ordered through booksellers or by contacting:

WestBow Press
A Division of Thomas Nelson & Zondervan
1663 Liberty Drive
Bloomington, IN 47403
www.westbowpress.com
1 (866) 928-1240

Because of the dynamic nature of the Internet, any web addresses or
links contained in this book may have changed since publication and may
no longer be valid. The views expressed in this work are solely those
of the author and do not necessarily reflect the views of the publisher,
and the publisher hereby disclaims any responsibility for them.

ISBN: 978-1-4908-6463-1 (sc)
ISBN: 978-1-4908-6465-5 (hc)
ISBN: 978-1-4908-6464-8 (e)

Library of Congress Control Number: 2014922967

Printed in the United States of America.

WestBow Press rev. date: 1/30/2015

This book is dedicated to the children of the new millennium

who know and understand the link with the Light

Contents

About the Author

Oliver H. Jobson was born in Falmouth, Jamaica. He attended The Priory School and later, boarding school at Munro College where he became the Cadet CSM, representing Jamaica in Cadets in Canada. This experience stimulated an interest in following a military career.

He received a scholarship to attend The Royal Military Academy Sandhurst, England, and as a career army officer, received a Queen's Commission. He served in the Jamaica Regiment, retiring as a Battle Group Commander after 11 years.

After retiring his Commission Oliver pursued entrepreneurial interests spanning industries such as entertainment, farming, hospitality, procurement, and international trade where he sat as a director on many boards.

A Roman Catholic by upbringing and a Christian Mystic by practice, he began reading the Bible and many spiritual books from the age of ten. As an adult Oliver spent many years traveling the world on a Spiritual quest to identify the common factor in all religions over which so many wars were fought in the name of God.

As an adult his travels required exploring the

Religion and Philosophy of each of the countries in which he visited. His research led him on many adventures: through the holy sites of Machu Picchu and Nazca in Peru; The Thor and Stonehenge in England; Lourdes in France, the mysteries of Indonesia; Monasteries of China, the Holy Lands of Israel, and the philosophies of India.

For many decades Oliver humbled himself at the feet of many Priests, Rabbis, Gurus, Yogis and Sri Sathya Sai Baba of Puttaparthi, absorbing their teachings and experiencing decades of continuous introspection, meditation, prayer, and practice.

He is a past member of the Ancient Free and Accepted Masons, Rotary, AMORC, and other associations. His many interests include soccer, Ontology, backgammon, music, and travel.

He is married, with two children and four grandchildren and currently resides in Miami, Florida with his wife Marcia.

Oliver H. Jobson is the author of *Expanding The Boundaries Of Self Beyond The Limit Of Traditional Thought,* and shares his knowledge on Meditation, Advaita Philosophy, and stress relief management techniques.

Preface

Jobson's second book, **Saved from Suicide by The Lord's Prayer**, presents a biographical testimonial on his relationship with a Source of Energy that manifests in his life at critical times, saving him from the possibility of death. It is this extraordinary Energy that intervened, literally diverting him from ending his life by suicide.

Throughout the book, Jobson describes frequent and interesting experiences that provide intrigue and bewilderment in an adventure found more in fantasy than in real life. His story commenced during his adolescent years as an acolyte in the Roman Catholic Church then moved on to other interesting anecdotes of his time in high school in Jamaica, in England, including experiences while attending The Royal Military Academy Sandhurst.

The story relates how from his youthful days Oliver subdued his ego, opening his mind to the teachings of Jesus Christ, as found in the New Testament. He honed in on a mission to prove the existence of a Creator by adhering to these teachings and offering his life to this extraordinary Source.

The depth of his spirituality and the strength of his

faith are evident in the book. Prayer and meditation are his constant means of communion as he draws strength and guidance from that Source that gives him a sense of balance, peace, and direction.

In his new book, Jobson shares the many pressures of having a series of challenges, occurring concurrently over a short period of time, that drove him into a depression, leading to his contemplation of suicide.

Pressures such as being detained by the security forces, having been made *persona non grata* with his government after leaving the army, the misfortunes of his businesses, the illness and death of his mother, marital problems, and financial loss; here is where the impact of his story takes place.

An exciting, intriguing, humorous book with short chapters that is difficult to put down. Well worth the read.

ONE

Serve To Lead

The Lord's Prayer or the Our Father has interested me from my youthful days, when I was but a 12-year-old acolyte at Sts. Peter and Paul Roman Catholic Church. I did not know why I had this interest in the Pater Noster, the Latin name of the prayer, but it somehow held an intriguing fascination that I would not have fathomed, were it not for an earlier experience, which I will relate later.

In those days, the Mass was always conducted in Latin, and that may have been the intrigue, although I knew the English translation by heart. Understanding Latin was not a problem as, at the time, Latin was a mandatory subject in school.

For those of you who have never been exposed to Latin, I am going to share the Pater Noster with you.

Pater noster qui es in coelis,

sanctificetur Nomen tuum.

Adveniat regnum tuum.

Fiat voluntas tua,

sicut in coelo et in terra.

Panem nostrum quotidianum da nobis hodie,

et dimitte nobis debita nostra

sicut et nos dimittimus debitoribus nostris.

Et ne nos inducas in tentationem,

sed libera nos a malo. Amen

It is a prayer which has always held a special meaning in my heart. Common sense or intuition made me realize that apart from being called The Lord's Prayer, and due to the length and intricacy of its verses, it had to have some terrific meaning and explanation. So that prayer naturally became my favorite to ponder on whenever I said it.

I went to boarding school when I was six and left when I was eight as we had moved from the country to the city where I attended a day school for a few years. I eventually went back to boarding school when I was about 15-years-old.

In general, I enjoyed boarding school. I liked sports and was a member of the school's rifle-shooting team; I was also in the Cadets (similar to ROTC). Nevertheless, I counted the days, weeks, semesters till I graduated, as I was eager to leave school and make an indelible mark in life.

However, my mom and dad forgot to remind me that on leaving school I had to get a job, pay taxes, find my own path in life, and pay my own way... just a slip of the memory I guess!

It was natural for us teenagers, at that time, to believe that life was a bed of roses all the time since we always had it so easy, apart from the strict discipline we received. I yearned for the day when I would grow up and become an adult so that I could earn my own way through life.

As a student, in that time period, most of our parents were strict, controlling, and dictatorial. We may not have liked the rules, but we respected our parents and followed their instructions and never thought for a second to be rude or even to disobey them. I would never have dreamed of hurting my mother, verbally, emotionally, or otherwise.

Come to think of it, we were better off for that rigid upbringing as it made us stable, strong, respectful individuals.

As soon as I left high school, I got a job with a general insurance company and, after comprehensive training in all departments, I became responsible for calculating all the payments for our clients' employees seeking Workmen's Compensation benefits.

Obviously, I had a Tariff to guide me, but the calculations did get complicated when someone lost two fingers on one hand and the thumb on the other hand. Basically, I had to apply a fair amount of common sense in working out the compensation.

The Workmen's Compensation Department was my post and dealing with the clients was my task. I am not sure if it were because I was young, fit, and fearless, or whether I was just a scapegoat to take the wrath and venomous anger that people spewed at what they felt was inadequate compensation for their specific accident.

The staff at the insurance company loved me, and they all smiled at my way of pacifying situations and getting out of them unscathed. This was not a frequent occurrence but, no matter what compensation was paid out, it was never enough for recipients. So these complaints generally provided entertaining drama for the other members of staff.

For example, the most severe occurrence was when a huge six-foot-four hulk of a metal worker with a bad temper and a short fuse, who had muscle ripping out of his working shirt came to my desk.

He spoke with fire spewing from his mouth like a dragon, and sparks of spittle flying in every direction of my face; he was completely cheesed off at the compensation I told him he was entitled to.

Actually, I thought he was going to chew me up like gum and turn the place upside down. Well, let me tell you that I knew I was physically fit but not suicidal, so I cringed to take him on. However, as with everything else in life, kind words, a genuine smile, and a humble attitude always disarms or neutralizes a bad situation.

I became seasoned to complaints as, in real Spiritual terms, I prayed for protection and was insured by the Light of God. Inspiration is a gift because a nervous smile and a kind word from a young lad usually makes a difference.

I left the insurance company after working for a year doing repetitious, monotonous, dreary work. It was not very rewarding, and seldom did we have such extreme, dramatic instances of excitement taking place to brighten up the time for me. But this particular experience led me to realize that I had another calling for a different adventure, and the armed forces provided that medium.

Having graduated from high school as the CSM (Company Sergeant Major), the most senior non-commissioned rank one could hold at high school, in Cadets. I knew at that time that I wanted to join one of the forces, so I contemplated on the choices open to me such as the Fleet Air Arm, RAF, British Army, or Canadian Forces.

Finally, I made an application to join the army as a Commissioned Officer and hoped I would be selected, with a scholarship, to attend Military School.

Although thousands of individuals applied, only one hundred were chosen to do the three-day recruitment test and selection board which consisted of a number of tests such as endurance, initiative, leadership, civics, and etiquette and included an overnight stay at the Officers' Mess where we had a formal dinner to see how refined we were at dining in such a setting and to check the quality of conversations we held on such formal occasions.

In those days, for selection into the Officer Corp, once we had the academic qualification, the whole exercise was arranged to see how much OQ (Officer Qualities) we had to be invited to join such an elite group of men. In short, our polish or refinement had to be impeccable for us to be members of such an august group of Officers and Gentlemen.

This refinement, in that era, was mostly gained from the upbringing and training at home. In retrospect, the Officer Corp represented the top three percent of the countries' brains and intellect and were the *crème de la crème* of the society. Intellect, integrity, fair-play and being a gentleman were the hallmarks of an Officer.

Finally, I was one of only two individuals selected from so many applicants. The great news was that we were being given scholarships to attend The Royal Military Academy Sandhurst (RMAS) in the United Kingdom.

It was a wonderful feeling getting this scholarship to attend the RMAS, a Military School that was regarded as the most prestigious Military Academy in the world. This was an amazing privilege; but first, the custom was to join

11

the army as ordinary soldiers do, as a private, with the understanding that we would be taken through many stages of progression in our training. Failure in any one of the courses would result in the instant loss of the scholarship.

The pressure was great, the responsibility heavy, the objective serious. The courses we had to pass were from the stage of a recruit to passing the Corporal's course, then the Sergeant's training and then the Sergeant Major's training. If we passed these courses our attendance was confirmed.

Believe me, it was not easy in those days as, in addition to the challenge, we were physically and verbally abused by the Non-Commissioned Officers (NCOs) such as our training Corporals and Sergeants and we had to have the guts to go through it with the stamina and grit expected from us, since we were geared to become officers trained to lead the same men who were training us.

We arrived at Sandhurst in Surrey, England, and as fate would have it, we began our training and studies in the autumn which gave us a gradual introduction to the coming winter season. It was a tough few years that bordered between sweet and sour, very much like a Chinese dish. Sour because of the rigorous academic and physical training but sweet because of the friends we made and the camaraderie among us all.

Sandhurst was a solid training school where we were taught mental, emotional and physical endurance, and stamina that gave us all an indomitable spirit as we learned to appreciate the motto of the Academy, *Serve To Lead.*

A very exhilarating time for me was the anticipation of and longing for winter to arrive. I did not in my wildest dreams imagine the temperature could get so cold. We see it on television, we imagine it intellectually, but we can never really conceive it until we experience it. I had never seen snow before and I can quite clearly remember being in the middle of a Military History class when it first started snowing that winter.

I just could not take my eyes off the beauty and wonder; at seeing those snowflakes fall, blanketing the ground in a covering of beautiful, white carpet. The Lecturer noticed my inattention to the class and, surprisingly, he suspended the class for five minutes and permitted me to run outside and experience it for the first time. I subsequently found out that the British Cadets and the Lecturer were entertained by the fact that it was my first experience.

Another incident occurred a few weeks later. We were out on a military exercise and we had to sleep in the snow for a few nights. Believe me, coming from the warm, white-sand beaches of the Tropics, I wondered if I were crazy to have accepted this scholarship.

Anyway, on this exercise my friend Peter, an English cadet, and I did an early stint on sentry duty and therefore, had the rest of the night to sleep. So true to form, we used our ground sheets to build a two-man bivouac.

It was freezing cold and as the night wore on, the colder it got. As both Peter and I were in this mini tent, we expected our body heat to keep us warm. The problem was that we were not that warm and Peter suggested that we hug each other to sleep.

I must point out here that I am far from being ho-mophobic, as my parents trained me well, besides I am far too masculine to be threatened by the thought of other people's sexual orientation. But coming from a small so-ciety, how could I honestly hug a man while we slept. It was unheard of!

As the night wore on and it got colder and colder and my feet got numb and then number - and I am sure Peter's did too - it got to the point where vanity was thrown out the window, and the principles of survival tripped in. So, subduing the ego and putting pride aside, I said, "Hey Pete, that suggestion you made about hugging each other sounded like a terrific idea to stay warm" - to which he was still in agreement. So I said, "Turn around and hug me."

We both had a quiet laugh.

Years later, Peter was killed in a theater of war. May your soul find the Light, my friend.

I could go on giving anecdotes of my time at Sandhurst but that would be another book in itself.

A few years later, I passed out - the British term for graduating - from the RMA Sandhurst. We were fortunate to have Field Marshal The Right Honourable The Viscount Montgomery of Alamein KG, GCB, DSO, PC., represent the Queen and take the salute at our Commissioning Parade.

Approximately 12 years later, I applied to retire my Commission as a Battle Group Commander or as is known in the United Kingdom and Commonwealth Countries, a Company Commander; it was accepted and I went into private enterprise.

TWO

Leadership by Example

On leaving the army, I began campaigning for the opposition political party; this did not sit very well with the socialist government in power at the time. It was also during election time, and the soldiers whom I had previously commanded in my Battle Group - which will now be referred to as my Company - consisting of over 120 men, all voted for the party for which I campaigned.

This action did not surprise me, as I knew the mental and moral connection I had in a military structure of men I had commanded with respect, discipline, fairness, and psychology. I had also made the motto of my Company,

We Lead by Example, and had trained my men in martial arts.

However, although I suspected that a few might follow my example, I did not expect them all to do so, considering my replacement had had command of them for eight months.

In response to my soldiers' unexpected display of exceptional loyalty to me, the army disbanded my Company and dispersed my men throughout different sections of the Force, thereby, neutralizing or negating my influence.

It is reasonable to appreciate that in the eyes of the army, this loyalty would have created a breach in security as that type of command relationship could be considered the nucleus of a potential coup.

The ludicrous thing is that I was, by no means, a political idealist, power crazy, stupid, or disloyal to the army and government I once served. Besides, I had other priorities and objectives in life that were void of politics.

It was obvious during those socialist years of politics, that the military hierarchy and government leaders were all paranoid, as they seemingly checked the votes of my soldiers, and probably read every one of their incoming and outgoing letters as well, as in those years email and the computer were not yet commercial instruments.

That experience, I daresay, was the greatest and most flattering compliment paid to any army officer. To think that the men I no longer commanded still respected me and trusted my judgment and the choices I made was, indeed, a blessing for which I was truly thankful.

I am blessed to have come from a business-oriented family, and my parents had many staff members and workers with whom I interfaced; so, in all my years of military life, I was never obsessed with the fact that I was in command of soldiers.

At the Royal Military Academy Sandhurst, we were given the very best of training including leadership of personnel and situations in both tactical and strategic command. Sandhurst prepared its potential officers to think as world leaders, as many are now.

I never threatened my soldiers with punishment using sections of the Manual of Military Law or the Queen's Regulations, nor did I ever get familiar with them. However,

I did treat them with due respect as their ages ranged from teenage to as old as my father.

I also had a policy that I never took kindly to lies, as the truth would always be better, no matter the consequences. I tried my very best to impart to my men a sense of trust, fairness, good judgment, ethics, and morals.

Anyway, you must realize that although I was dismayed at the fact that the army disbanded my Company and deployed the soldiers elsewhere, I was extremely perturbed that they had completely destroyed a fighting unit I had spent so much time building and molding. It was my baby and I was proud of it!

So, in my disappointment, I turned, as I usually do, to some comforting philosophy - Ecclesiastes 3: *"To everything there is a season, and a time to every purpose under the heaven..."*

By then, I had become *persona non grata* on every military compound in the country. I was now relegated to being a subversive individual. In reality, that perception probably stemmed from the fact that although I was sympathetic to the plight of the poor, I was very opposed to having Castro send troops from Cuba to help with training the army. How could I have condoned such a thing, when I had always regarded communism as the enemy of civilized man? This idea of some people being more equal than others just did not work for me.

The effort to demean me resulted in the army making a surprise raid on my house, searching for illegal weapons and subversive materials. Needless to say, they found nothing worthwhile, but the raid was a traumatic experience for my wife, daughter, and my son.

THREE

The Value of Good Management

As a retired army officer, I had a very active social life, living next door to a Deputy Commissioner of Police on one side, a medical doctor on the other side, a quantity surveyor and author across the road and other professionals along the way. Actually, we lived on a cul-de-sac, so we practically *owned* the area - until my house was raided.

I went to work at a multinational corporation as the Logistics Supervisor at the invitation of the managing director, who had a logistic problem that needed sorting out, so I took the challenge.

Working there was a terrific experience! The

company was very well run, the working environment was most pleasant, and the staff was one big family; everyone had a sense of involvement and commitment to the company.

One day, to add a spark of *entertainment* to my work-day, at 0800 hours, two well-dressed men in suits walked into my office and identified themselves as plainclothes detectives of senior rank, presenting their IDs.

They apologized profusely for the intrusion and embarrassment, and told me they were instructed to invite and escort me to the Criminal Investigation Bureau (CIB), but first, they had to relieve me of my firearm, ammunition, and passport.

I extracted my firearm, which was concealed under my jacket, and told them I had to go to my house for the bulk of my ammunition and my passport. With an air of support and cooperation they drove me home, where I retrieved the items.

It is necessary to interject here and share a disappointing experience with you. You never know your true *friends* until a time of crisis occurs! It is difficult to illustrate to you the number of people I knew and the vast number of friends I had at the time.

Modestly speaking, I was very popular and extremely well-known, so every weekend my home was blessed with a number of friends visiting. We laughed and joked with each other and had deep, intellectual, stimulating conversations on many different topics.

However, when my house was raided and the news spread, my friends became paranoid, and as they certainly did not want to be subjected to the same experience, they all stopped visiting. Every one became scared of the government, as during this period, actually a few months before the elections, a State of Emergency was declared and many members of the opposition party, as well as those who spoke against the government, were arrested under trumped-up charges.

Back to my story - after being taken out of my office so early in the morning, I spent the entire day, until late evening, being interrogated on ridiculous accusations. I do not wish to go through the whole enchilada of questioning I endured, as this information is for the sole purpose of taking you through the events in my life to culminate in the title on this book. However, overall, the day was intense, amusing, and entertaining - to say the least.

In retrospect, I was placed under surveillance by

the security forces from the day I began campaigning for the opposition party, so I felt as if I had my personal bodyguard following me everywhere, which I thought was ideal as it was a security expense that was not coming out of my pocket.

The executive management of the company heard about the ordeal I was having, especially of me being in the bad books of the government because I was vehemently against communism or a socialism that bordered on, or close to, communism.

My managing director was aware of the number of threats I was receiving warning me to cease campaigning, and getting involved in politics with the opposition party.

It was during this period of harassment that an executive from head office was visiting our branch. He met with me and explained that as I was held in high regard, he could have me transferred to another country if my family was being harassed and I felt threatened or scared for my life.

I was very touched by this gesture; it was thoughtful, kind, and considerate. I voiced my appreciation telling him that it was not my nature to run away; instead I would stay and be the last to leave, *turning off the lights* in the process, if necessary.

When we speak about a family of employees, when we speak about executives caring for the morale of the staff, when we speak about taking care of the welfare of staff, then we are speaking about excellent corporations that grew and expanded at a rapid rate in those days.

I wish to pay particular tribute to the quality and caliber of executive management of the past, as it makes a tremendous difference to the staff when they realize that the management respects and values their contribution and covers their back.

Management and leaders of companies, at that time, were quite aware that the staff made the company. With the dedicated contribution from a staff whose morale is high, a company will move from strength to strength. The staff's loyalty and service to the company is directly proportionate to the value placed on the staff. So, if they are only regarded as numbers, I leave you to imagine what the company will have in return.

To get the maximum efficiency from workers their psychological welfare must be well recognized and addressed.

FOUR

Changing the Garment
When it is Time

I am not sure if you would regard this as a great privilege or a misfortune of fate, if you believe in that sort of thing; but whether you see the glass as half-full or as half- empty, it has been a terrific learning experience for me. What I am referring to is the fact that I have witnessed the passing of many people, both naturally and tragically.

The first, and most significant, experience was the passing of my grandmother, Rhoda Craig, who had been living with us for many years. In my culture, parents are revered and if, when, and where possible, when the parents are old, there is always a place for them in the homes of their children.

This usually turns out to be mutually beneficial because the grandparents pick up the slack in many ways: by helping with the cooking of meals, keeping the place tidy, and even doing laundry. However, most importantly, they take the place of a nanny for the kids, which allows the discipline, custom, culture, family knowledge, and history to be passed on to the next generation.

So, by the time my strong, upbeat grandmother - who shall be referred to from now on as Mama - passed on, I had learned many lessons. We were taught to obey adults when we were spoken to or called, not so much because it was an ego trip, but as a matter of respect and concern. This ancient wisdom came to pass and I was there to witness it.

Mama was in bed, as she had the flu, and had not been feeling very well for a few days. She called my mother in a gentle tone of love, just once, and my mother immediately responded by going to her bedroom to see what she wanted. Mama asked for a glass of water, which my mother got her immediately.

At the time, I was only 11-years-old, and I followed my mother, whom Mama called Mae, to the room; she gave the water to Mama who took a sip, handed my mother the glass, said thank you, and in the next breath said, "Mae, I am gone." She then fell back on the bed. She had passed away.

Obviously, I was very sad she had gone, as I loved her so much, but deep down I knew it was only her body that had left as her words, her guidance, her love, her kindness, and gentleness would always live on in my memory.

But, the most remarkable thing happened to me that night. I had gone to bed crying, still feeling sad, and eventually I tried to sleep. Mama appeared to me and I held her, kissed her and said, "Mama, what are you doing here? You are supposed to be dead."

She said, "No my darling, I am not dead, I am very much alive. I only left my body behind."

On hearing her say this I got extremely excited and hugged and kissed her again; at which point, she disappeared and I fell into a deep sleep, feeling satisfied that she would always be there with me - all I had to do was call her.

As I got older, I witnessed the passing of four uncles, maternal and paternal. Time passed, and I saw the deaths of many people; for example, while driving over the mountains one evening, I discovered that a bus, with approximately 40 passengers, had skidded off the wet, slippery road and tumbled down a fifty-foot precipice. I stopped to assist, along with a friend who was traveling with me that evening.

It was not a pretty sight! All the passengers had been thrown from the bus. Eight of them had been decapitated, and various body parts of other passengers were scattered around, and I had to place these parts on the deceased individuals to whom they belonged. Eventually, many ambulances arrived to deal with the situation.

I have omitted many gory details of a number of the deaths I have seen, both in and out of the army. By the time I was 23, I had even buried by best friend, John, who had been in a very bad accident and I dissuaded his parents from identifying his body as he was in such very bad condition.

He lived on the summit of a mountain and the way to his home was on a very narrow road with an extremely deep precipice of perhaps a thousand feet on one side.

The British custom is to drive on the left, and the precipice was on the left side as he ascended.

That particular evening, he was on his way home when he drove too close to the edge, possibly because there may have been a car descending the mountain and he moved too far over to the left causing his car wheels to slip off the road and he cartwheeled over the precipice.

Unfortunately, he was not wearing his seat belt and was thrown from the car, landing on a ledge, and the car rolled on top of him. This snow-white man with blond hair died from asphyxiation, causing his whole body to turn black from suffocation.

When I was 33, I was subjected to a most traumatic experience. I had been in Florida skydiving, when it was revealed to me, in a dream, that my very healthy mother, whom I lovingly called Mumsie, would die on December 14, the day before my sister's birthday. At that time, my sister lived in New York.

I made the necessary arrangements and returned home to see my mother just before December 13. On December 14, she was admitted to hospital for observation, as x-rays had revealed, what appeared to have been, a shadow on her lungs. This observational visit resulted in a longer stay than was expected by other members of the family.

I remembered the dream and it made me realize at the time that this hospital visit could be the precursor to her death.

It actually was a mixed period of time for me. My commercial fishing business was going through a challenging time. I had been warned, initially, about investing in only one fishing vessel to do commercial fishing. I was told it was best to buy two vessels so, if one broke down or got laid up for some reason, I still would have a cash-flow going with the second boat.

However, being young and feeling invincible, I had decided to take a chance. I started the business with one boat, as I could not think of a good reason why the vessel would stop working, for any cause. So, off I went on my new adventure.

FIVE

The Pressure was Great

Sorting out the logistics issue at the multinational corporation took eight months, at the end of which I was asked to remain with the company, but I wanted to try my hand at a new adventure, such as commercial fishing. I acquired a fishing vessel and needed to find a competent and qualified captain and crew. It took me some time to find them, as I changed about forty crew members before acquiring the final crew.

Finally, I had a good captain and five efficient crew members with whom I was very satisfied.

Whenever my friends asked why I decided to go into the fishing business, I always replied that Jesus

Christ said, "Follow Me, and I will make you fishermen." That was my motivating force, until I re-read the New Testament.

When we do not take sound advice from the older professionals, who know business better, then we pay the price for our mistakes. As I stated in my book - *Expanding the Boundaries of Self Beyond the Limit of Traditional Thought* – "he who feels it, knows it."

Whenever the boat came in from sea, it brought in at least five tons of fish, which is exactly what the market wanted, at the time. I sold to fish vendors, restaurants, and supermarkets. The boat came in about twice a month after spending approximately two weeks at sea on each trip. As soon as the cargo was off-loaded, the vessel was replenished and out it went again.

I soon realized the wisdom of having two boats. In the event that one boat was laid up, the other would provide protection against the need to have a continuous cash flow available. I also discovered the major factor hindering my ability to make money in this venture, which you may find bizarrely amusing.

After completing the day's fishing and returning to base, the captain's *friends* would meet him at sea and he would sell them some of my prize catch; he would then pay off the crew to keep quiet. Unknown to the captain, the crew had their own techniques to keep some of the fish for themselves. So if the skipper didn't *take you for a ride*, the crew did. Pilfering and tall tales seemed a part of their DNA.

With all the checks and systems I put in place, to this day I cannot explain to you how the captain or crew were able to filter off at least ten percent of the cargo. I felt like the cat who had been totally confused by the mice. It is said that sometimes the hands can move faster than the eyes can see.

Anyway, there were many other factors that impeded my chances of making a profit, which I had not foreseen in my business plan and, believe me, they all happened. I tasted the effects of Murphy's Law over a period of two years. If the weather was severe and the seas were rough, it was not advisable to sail, so we could not go to sea.

That was by no means all. One day, five fishermen were getting a ride back to the mainland with me, as they lived on the Cays, approximately 100 miles at sea, where they did their own fishing. On that evening, the engineer on the boat overslept, the two engines overheated from a lack of oil, and one literally exploded around two o'clock in the morning.

I must point out that it was one of those nights with absolutely no moonlight; everything was pitch black, but for the light from the boat. Although this was a costly mishap for my pocket, it was, in retrospect, quite humorous for the following reason.

To my shock, on hearing the explosion all the fishermen jumped up, frightened, thinking the boat was sinking and ran up on deck ready to jump, taking up a diving stance. I quickly shouted out to them, "What are you guys doing? Don't jump if you can't swim."

There was dead silence!

My next question was, "Can any of you swim?"

Out of the silence came, in unison, "No Captain, we can't."

"It would be impossible to find you guys in the sea on such a dark night, so stay put," I snickered.

After their fright and panic subsided, I told them, "The boat has only blown one engine, and I have no intention of diving into the sea to save any of you, no matter how much I love you."

Luckily, with patience, we made it home on the other engine.

After that episode, I decided to change the engines to two 471-GMs and they made a big difference in performance. Over the two years of my fishing ordeal, I had a few other mishaps.

I was out with the boat to ensure that none of my cargo was being pilfered. We were anchored approximately two hundred yards from the Cays, in about 50 feet of water, some ninety miles at sea, from the base. It was twilight, just at that time when you can actually see and feel life/nature, coming awake.

I was deep in sleep when my engineer came to tell me that the boat seemed to be sinking. At a quick glance, the boat did look a bit low, or maybe, I should have said that the water had come into the vessel and to my surprise, the level did seem too close to my bunk.

The first place I checked was the cargo hold and yep, the fish were all floating. Trying to keep my cool, I checked the engine room and my two 471-GM engines were submerged. I was now very concerned, as the nearest vessel was about a mile away.

However, we did have a lifeboat on board. The

thing that really bothered me was the 60 or 70 hungry-looking sharks that normally swam around the boat, waiting for us to throw spoiled fish into the sea, or for one of us to accidentally fall overboard.

A quick story about sharks - who said sharks are not intelligent? On one occasion a number of fishermen came in their canoes to my boat to sell me fish and the sharks were all swimming about their canoes.

This *smart* fisherman decided that he would be mean to a shark and hit its snout with his machete. The shark turned around and swam out some distance, then returned swimming fast towards the fisherman's canoe and hit it with such force that the canoe capsized and we had to quickly get the fisherman from out of the water.

With some positive thinking and powerful prayer, I started the GM engines, even though they were under water; turned on the bilge pumps, and with time and patience sucked the water out of the boat, which nicely refloated. Fortunately, the two alternators and batteries were stored much higher than the engines which allowed me to accomplished the miracle of refloating the boat.

At the rate at which the water was seeping into the boat, I figured it was one of the plates on the steel hull that was leaking, so I told the crew to join the other vessel at sea and I would take the boat back to base by myself.

My crew would hear of no such thing, and although I ordered them to go, they refused to leave me saying that if I went under, then they would go under, as well.

I was very concerned that if it were a crack in one of the plates and we sank, even with the life vests we had on board, there was always the possibility that someone would have drowned. My crew was very supportive, and I slowly traveled at three knots per hour back to base.

On returning, I put the vessel on dry-dock only to discover that the plates were fine but we had sprung a leak in the propeller shaft gland. I also seized the opportunity and had my Borg Warner gear boxes overhauled.

During my adult life, I spent a considerable amount of quality time reading the New Testament, meditating and praying for enlightenment. For those who do not know, there is a huge difference between the last two topics.

My whole quest, from childhood, has been to do two things spiritually. First, is to find the Universal God under whose jurisdiction all religions and all matters in the Universe fall. Second, is to find the Truth as Jesus Christ meant it. Not as man interpreted His teachings, according to our ego and limited understanding.

Hence, I was adamant about discovering and understanding the teachings of Jesus Christ. I have not mentioned this before, as it was not necessary to state that most of my thoughts are about God, as saying so seems very condescending and overbearing.

But what I can share with you is that every thought I have, everything I say, and do, I do as a sacrifice to the Lord in expectation that, in time, the answers to all my questions will be revealed.

To achieve this end, I had to stay centered and balanced, and rise above the organized chaos and confusion that I appeared to have been experiencing at the same period. I fervently prayed for wisdom, strength, and guidance.

SIX

Meandering through a
Maze of Confusion

The power of prayer never ceases to amaze me! When we pray for spiritual gifts, when we pray for our daily bread, when we pray for those intangible things that will make us better and nobler human beings, our prayers are usually answered; if not immediately, then in due course.

I have always tried to live my life as a living prayer. I am not implying that I am a saint, far from it, but I have tried my best to live my life in such a manner that I can serve as an incentive for another to glorify God. I have done my utmost to live, not as a dogmatic, religious parrot repeating words and phrases from the Bible that I do not understand, but to live as a spiritual being.

I never have to convince or declare to anyone that I am a Christian, as to me, people who do that seem as if they have an ulterior motive, or are trying to prove to themselves that they are godly.

If you are sincere and honest you do not have to broadcast your affiliation, as your behavior and words will reflect who you are. The Light needs no justification as illumination radiates from all places and all situations, no matter now negative or evil the situation may be.

Many people have asked me what is the difference between Religion and Spirituality, as I am often saying that I am far from being religious, but I am spiritual.

To help others to know the difference, I have explained and coined a definition of the difference between the two words in the following manner:

Spirituality comes from within the memory and consciousness of the soul, which never dies. Spirituality is a natural feeling of well-being and a state of appreciation for all forms of life.

Religion is a dogma and ritual created and

introduced by man for the spiritual discipline and the so-cial well-being of mankind.

Spirituality is natural while Religion is social. Hence, spirituality originates from within our soul, religion was created by man and introduced to man for man's benefit.

I had every trust in the Lord Jesus Christ that the answers to all my prayers would be revealed from the mere fact that some time in the past at Sunday School I had experienced the Lord telling me that He was no longer on the cross. I was about ten-years-old, or close to that age, so as far as I was concerned, I had my first personal connection and experience with the Lord.

Mumsie's indefinite stay in the hospital to do a se-ries of tests, proved a real interesting challenge. I made it a point of duty, borne from love, to visit her daily and spend a few hours chatting with her about issues, expe-riences, events, and family. What made this unique is that although we had spoken about these things over the years, the privilege of being able to bond with her in the hospital, drew us closer and increased the impact of our love for each other.

Over the three months she spent in the hospital, I slept in her room many nights; particularly when I sensed that she wanted me to stay with her. Our conversations were many and varied. We spent time talking about faith, religion, spirituality, life, and death. As her stay grew longer, she became weaker and weaker, and her vital signs dipped so low the doctor told me, on many occasions, to "bid her farewell."

Although it started months before Mumsie was admitted to hospital, my wife and I were having our issues. At the time, we had the most adorable children one could have. Our daughter was the older and the apple of my eye, and I took her everywhere with me.

It was as if she were my mascot, and all my staff treated her like a little princess. But that did not change the fact that my wife and I were just not seeing eye to eye. We were going through an emotionally rough patch and we both realized that it was just a matter of time before we parted.

"That which hath been is now; and that which is to be hath already been, and God requireth that which is past." Ecclesiastes 3: v 15.

I am convinced that some things in life are just meant to happen! I call it a happening! It is an act of fate, and nothing can be added to it nor taken from it. It is a quantum experience that is written in the blueprint of consciousness. To me, fate is the sum total of Karmic experiences that co-ordinate, harmonize, come together, or intersect, causing certain inevitable things to happen.

This happening may be negative or positive, depending on the way you perceive life. In my first book, I wrote a chapter on Karma to help those who do not know or understand about it.

The union between my first wife, the mother of my children, and me was a learning experience from which we both gained a lot physically, mentally, emotionally, socially, intellectually, and spiritually. The divorce proved to be a traumatic experience for our daughter, but not our son, as he was just a little baby, too young to have grown accustomed to having his dad around.

The amazing thing was that my wife and I never, ever quarreled; we never raised our voices at each other. But, subconsciously, we knew that the end of our marriage was drawing nigh.

It is surprising how life takes on a different tone when we live a spiritual life, putting into practice all the teachings we have learned over the years and still continue to learn. An interesting tenet of hers was that it took two to quarrel, so she never incited anger in me.

I learned to exercise discipline and self-control - it's called Yoga of the Mind and Spirit - which also includes the discipline of Love; unlike Hatha which *"calms the mind's agitation temporarily, and may improve health and prolong life for a few more years."* ~Sri Sathya Sai Baba.

It is so easy for the ego to take over and control the emotions. The ego never enjoys harmony and feeds on negative emotion, it is what is regarded as the devil. Therefore, a spiritual person also knows that the ego becomes the devil, if allowed to run wild. It is like having an untrained, viciously-cross dog on a leash, then letting it loose in a public place; it would just go wild, biting people and wantonly causing havoc.

In retrospect, the fact that the chapter on our marriage was coming to a close, coupled with many other painful experiences I was having, made me realize that there are no chances or coincidences in this life.

As is written and frequently repeated by others, everything happens for a reason; likewise, everything happens in Divine order, or by cosmic design. The answer to all synergistic experiences comes as a result of Karmic influences. This is why God never makes a mistake.

Many times, those Karmic debts date way back and

are influenced by some action, or inaction, that may have originated many lifetimes ago. Whether you believe in re-incarnation, or not, is immaterial. It is a natural, metaphysical, and cosmic law which transcends the dimensions.

The more I think about the mathematical disposition of Karma on a quantum level, the more often I marvel at the greatness and magnificence of this God. Just think. God is such a Creator, such a Physicist that this Karmic program has been set in motion to deal with any and every circumstance we may think of; whether it is verbal, physical, emotional, or practical. Karma is seen throughout the universe as cause and effect.

Karma accounts for any action, tangible or intangible, that is taken by anyone, anywhere, in this or any dimension, and it will always have a consequential effect.

Karma, simply put, is the name given to the law that Jesus Christ spoke about: "...*for whatsoever a man soweth, that shall he also reap."* It is cause and effect; also, it is Newton's third law that states *"for every action, there is an equal and opposite reaction."*

This is why God is the Eternal Witness. He is to me - for the lack of a more descriptive word – male, female, and neuter gender. He is the Divine Energy or Light behind creation, and man becomes the Lord, one with God, when he is infused with that Energy, Light, Spirit or Holy Ghost, like Jesus Christ.

Therefore, God has set in motion various cosmic Laws, and we are told not to break them. We are instructed to strive for and follow the Light, the path of illumination. If not, we will be left to fend for ourselves in darkness and ignorance.

At the time Mumsie went into the hospital, my brother Max, and I, had a restaurant and cocktail lounge which was developing rather nicely. It was well supported and became a meeting place for friends and business associates. However, it was a secondary business for us, more like a hobby, as we already had our main businesses to deal with on a daily basis.

As the weeks passed, being there for Mumsie while attending to our main business, along with the involvement in the restaurant, became a big strain. It was just difficult juggling so many balls at the same time. Mumsie was the priority, so my brother Max, and I, gracefully backed out of the restaurant business.

SEVEN

Coming to a New Realization

A very important lesson in life is to have a sense of humor and never lose it. Unless you have a sense of humor, you can never understand how much it helps to make light of situations. My teacher in India, Sri Sathya Sai Baba, said that the best way to enlightenment is to loosen up; how true that is.

A sense of humor allows the most tense moments to be lightened; besides, laughing is, in itself, a very therapeutic exercise. Laughter is good for the heart and the blood pressure, laughter keeps you youthful, and it exercises the face muscles as well. I think humor could be a buffer against aging. Trust me, I know, I laugh all the time and no, I don't want your opinion about the wrinkles on my face!

As I said before, I spent many nights with Mumsie and she was a bit concerned that I was not, instead, at home with my family. However, her concern swiftly eased and left her teary-eyed when I quickly reassured her that my wife was very pleased I was spending these moments with her in hospital. We all did not know how long she had left on this beautiful planet. It is so very true that *"man's extremity is God's opportunity."* 2 Cor. 1.

Mumsie and I always shared a very close rapport mentally and intuitively. When I was at school in England, she always knew what was going on with me, and every time I called home, she could virtually tell me the issues before I mentioned them. It was almost as if she were expecting the calls.

A really peculiar thing happened during my last term at boarding school. This school was located far out in God's country, in the middle of nowhere, and situated on top of a mountain overlooking the plains on one side, and the sea on the other.

The buildings were made from cut-stone and were built in the 1800s. The school's motto, in Latin, is: *In arce sitam quis acultabit;* the general translation is: *a city on a hill cannot be hidden.*

There were the odd, *delinquent boys* who made it a habit to run away from school, so the headmaster had issued instructions that no public or private transportation should pick up any student who could not furnish a letter granting them permission to travel.

Needless to say, those were the days of corporal punishment; when we received three, six, or ten strokes, sometimes in front of all the student body, usually administered in the gymnasium, depending on how serious the offence was.

Can you just imagine how embarrassing and humiliating that was?

Mind you, everyone knew how strict this school was, so on the odd occasion the student who was being disciplined could be a hero to the younger ones if he didn't do much flinching at the stinging effect of each stroke.

These strokes were administered with a very thin, straight but flexible bamboo cane, that never seemed to break, and had the remarkable capacity to be bent in any direction without cracking - another wonderful application of the bamboo.

The school had many old ghost stories. Most evenings it was very misty, and as the strong winds blew, we could hear the willow trees whistling in the breeze on the mountaintop. For those with a vivid imagination, it certainly created an eerie feeling as we conjured up ghost stories, and the like, in our young minds.

From time to time, some boys claimed to have seen many spirits walking about at night, and others screamed at seeing headless ghosts holding their heads in their arms. I guess they could have written some good bedtime stories.

Since the drive was about three hours from my house to the college, my father gave me a lovely, burgundy Fiat Gordini four-door sedan. It was a dream car for me, at that time. Actually, my father didn't give me this car because he wanted to be as kind as he usually was to me, but because he was looking for a way out of driving me all that distance to school.

One particular holiday, I had a school friend visiting at home. He was from Sweden, and, like me, he was also a boarder. His name was Charles Stodberg and I have not seen him since school, bless his soul.

Just a few days before returning to school, we were

51

going to see some friends and I was driving at a considerable speed, I must say, when I had to negotiate a right-hand bend.

I was doing pretty well, changing down to a lower gear on my stick shift when, suddenly, while negotiating the corner, the car drove over sand on the asphalt from a previous shower of rain causing the vehicle to slide to the left, hitting the bank.

It happened so fast that I lost control when the car hit the curb. The momentum caused the car to roll over about three-and-a-half times, as if we were in a circus.

When the car came to a stop, resting on its roof, Charles crawled through the open window while I was still sitting upside down holding onto the steering wheel. Collecting my composure and up-righting myself, I too, crawled through the window and joined Charles on the road where we thumbed a ride home.

A family who happened to have been passing at the time and witnessed the accident picked us up and they were most surprised to see that we had suffered no serious injuries, just a small cut Charles had got on his knee.

Talk about a caring family, good Samaritans and concerned parents, they took us right home and both

Charles and I exited their car and walked in confidently, as if nothing had happened. As we were walking up the driveway, Mumsie came out and said, "Are you both hurt?"

My response was, "Why on earth would you ask such an outrageous question?"

"I was resting, and I saw your car rolling, not too long ago, so I know you overturned the car."

I couldn't hide anything from her as she *had my number;* we were too closely linked, spiritually. At that point, tears rolled down my cheeks, and I apologized to her and asked her not to tell Dad, as I was scared he would be angry.

My loving mother said, "I am so happy you are both alive and have not suffered any serious injury."

To my surprise, all my dad said was, "You have to try to drive more carefully," and that was the end of that episode. I must confess that he drove us back to school in good cheer.

EIGHT

A Moment of Stubbornness

*"It is always good to live in the present
and allow the future to catch up with us."*
~Oliver H. Jobson

With Mumsie still in the hospital, the weeks passed, the days and nights took a toll on me, and I had to give up the restaurant. My marriage was deteriorating fast and my fishing business was a challenge with one boat; it was losing money hand over fist.

It was during this period of severe introspection that I realized that Jesus Christ did NOT say "Follow Me, and I will make you fishermen." What he said was *"Follow Me, and I will make you fishers of men"* - a slight misunderstanding on my part, I daresay!

Almost to the detriment of my fishing business, I placed my priority on Mumsie. When I reflect on those days, and the time we spent chatting with each other, I do realize it was an extremely rare privilege for a son, or any child, to have such candid, forthright, loving conversations with their mother, especially prior to her transition.

Having been present at the passing of so many friends, family members, and acquaintances, I knew the symptoms to look for, which was evident in her case with the passage of time. As the day of reckoning drew closer, her eyes became glassy and I could see she was looking beyond, into the abyss.

I spoke with her about it and she confirmed that she was seeing the Light we always spoke about, and prayed to, and it was a joyful experience since I had reminded her what to expect.

Mumsie confirmed to me that her mother, father, brothers, and the other family members who had died, had appeared in the Light and were prepared to receive her, when she was ready. By this time, I knew that she was Astral projecting and mentally and spiritually preparing to make her final exit from the body.

Deep down, I also knew she was torn between leaving to meet the family members and staying to be with her children to whom she was so attached. It can be quite a devastating internal conflict when there are two opposing choices to make between life and death.

Something I learned from my spiritual teachings, particularly in India, was that, whether we want to believe it or not, we decide when we have ended our sojourn on this plain, in this dimension, and actually decide to move on. In fact, I believe many of us know roughly when we are going to depart. We may not know the how, but we do have a sense of the when.

That was the last night I slept at the hospital with my mother, as at about 11:00 p.m. she told me to call my brother and also my sister in New York and tell them to come.

Mumsie's vital signs had dropped extremely low on many occasions over the previous three months. On the odd occasion, she appeared to have slipped into a coma for a few moments causing the doctor to actually warn me saying: "This is it, the final moment, please say goodbye". But this was the first time in the three months that Mumsie had made such a demand of me.

Therefore I left the room to make the calls but because it was so late at night and the fact that I did not want to be an alarmist, I balked at the notion of waking either of my siblings, so although I had said I would, I really didn't call them.

When I got back to her room, to my surprise, she said to me, "You have not spoken to them yet because you have not called to give them my message. Why are you being so stubborn? This is most unlike you not to grant my wishes. Please go and call them."

Without further delay or hesitation, I went and fulfilled her wishes as instructed. Her ability to know that I had not made the call was as a result of her being in the Astral plain, in which dimension, time and space do not exist as everything just is. Hence, her ability to see my inaction although I was not within her eyesight.

I must admit that my mind was blown, as I was

speaking to her with reservation due to her weak condition, and at the same moment, she was able to tell me that both her son and her daughter were not aware of her request.

She could see me - she was not only with me in the physical body, she was with them spiritually, even though they were in two different countries. I should have known better because the Astral or spiritual body is not confined to, or limited by, time and space, as it functions in another continuum, another dimension.

When my brother and sister arrived that morning, I left them to spend those last moments with her, as I was blessed to have had so much of her for so long and she may have wanted to speak to each of them, privately.

I excused myself at about 12:30 p.m. and went home to check on the kids, as they were with the nanny - my wife being at work - and also to have a good shower, a home-cooked meal, and to sleep for a short while.

At about 3:30 p.m. Cathy, a family friend who frequently visited Mumsie in the hospital, called my landline at home to say Mumsie was fading fast, close to taking her last breath and I should come as quickly as possible.

It might have just been a few decades ago, but remember there were no cellular phones in those days.

I got dressed with a myriad thoughts rushing through my mind at the same time. Thoughts such as:

- *I was going to miss Mumsie taking her last breath.*
- *I would never see my mother alive again in this dimension.*
- *Should I rush to get there as the hospital was at least half-an-hour from my home; or would it be better for me to forfeit that privilege and stay home to pray for her soul to be guided to the Light?*

At that moment, I sat on the bed for a few seconds and at 4:00 p.m. I passed out for a few minutes on an Astral projection. On regaining my composure I eventually got to the hospital and was told that four o'clock was the exact time she passed. I realized then, that I must have accompanied her at the crossing between this dimension and the next.

I know that sounds very strange but I would not be surprised if you and many of your friends have been conscious of leaving your bodies and actually seen yourselves lying on your beds. If not, then I am pretty sure you have been lying down on the bed and jerked yourself awake.

The doctor will tell you it's a muscle spasm. My analysis is that on the odd occasion when you are just about to fall asleep, unconsciously you feel yourself losing control or leaving your body, as if you are floating away somewhere, and with a quick reflex prevent yourself from doing so.

Mumsie never wanted us to cry for her as she felt we should rejoice at her passing from this plain as there would be a rebirth for her in the next. So, as requested, I tried my very best to hold back the tears - with tremendous difficulty, unsuccessful as I was, I daresay, but at least I was disciplined with it.

Her memorial went off very well indeed, as it was more than just a funeral but a final tribute celebrating her life.

On her tombstone we wrote,

God's greatest gift returned to God
- our Mother.

NINE

A Cry for Help

Two months after my mother's passing, I had my thirty-third birthday. I was sad because I was young and I missed her. We never think about death until it is often too late; however, although we can never get another biological mother, whoever takes up the mantle to nurture us and show us the way and the values of and in life, is the earthly mother God sent us, as a gift.

On reassessing the situation over the previous two years, I was really in a quagmire. My fishing business was not doing well and the boat was leaking my dollars fast, so I closed the business down shortly after the memorial service.

My wife and I still had our issues, and I felt I was almost broke, and broken. In reality, I was just totally exhausted. A normal person would have taken a rest, but I never thought of it.

A very bad habit I had, at the time, was a desire for the taste of alcohol and the feeling of euphoria it brought, which did not help the situation; I was an alcoholic! I remember coming home late many evenings and feeling no pain. One night in particular after the boat docked, I drank with the crew and fishermen and imbibed too many drinks...more than normal. When I arrived home I realized then that I needed to take control of myself.

So, at two o'clock in the morning, I called Alcoholics Anonymous and when the person on the other end of the phone answered, I immediately hung up. I thought that if I could recognize the problem and admit to it, then I could cure myself as nothing in this world is supposed to control me; instead, I should be controlling it.

As the months passed, I eventually cut back on my drinking to a sociable level.

In reading over the previous paragraph, I thought that anyone reading it would imagine that I was a control freak, which was not so.

However, I must admit that when it comes to my person, I refuse to allow any outside factor to take control of me and, literally, possess me. I have always believed that my body is a temple, and I am the resident priest, so I had to make sure my control was from within, not from without.

Therefore, all the issues I was having, as well as the drinking, made me very depressed; and one after-noon, after playing with my daughter for a while - she was about four-years-old at the time - and then putting her to bed, I still felt very depressed, lost, and extremely sorry for myself.

I decided to do something about this depression so I went to the bedroom for my gun to end my life. Then I remembered - the government had seized my gun a few months before. Well, I must tell you, I was very angry with God, and I called Him a sneak and a deceitful God, as He knew fully well that my life would have come to this stage, and I would have wanted to end it; so in His Divine awareness He ensured that my gun was taken from me.

I then went to my bed, after refreshing myself, so I could have a clear head to decide on the next step to take, in the absence of my gun. My wife was fast asleep, so I lay on the bed and contemplated the idea of cutting my wrist, and where I would do it. I certainly did not want to create a big mess of blood for my wife and the maid to clean. Besides, I did not wish my kids to see me like that. In retrospect, I am amazed that I was more concerned about making a mess than taking my life!

Having spent almost 12 years in the army and attended the best Military Academy in the world, I never made idle threats, and had a principle that if it became necessary to point a gun at anyone, a bullet would come out the barrel. So, my desire to end my life was not a romantic idea, but was, obviously, incited from a fit of extreme weakness and depression.

Here is where my story gets better; here is where an extraordinarily inexplicable incident took place. In fact, at the time, I deemed it a Divine intervention, and still do. As I lay on the bed contemplating my next move, a telepathic voice, similar to the one I had heard as a kid, saying that Jesus was not on the cross, and the voice that saved me from many accidents said, "Pick up the Bible!"

I always had a copy of the King James Bible sitting on my night table, as I enjoyed reading the Psalms and the New Testament.

I picked up the Bible, as instructed. Then, the same familiar voice said, "Open it!"

This telepathic voice was a gentle, loving, soft but firm voice that, in retrospect, sounded more like a command. And so I did. That was the last I heard from the voice that evening. I must confess that ever since the Sunday School incident, that voice has guided me numerous times, and on many occasions it saved my life. I know I have been very blessed, and I have not forgotten it for a moment.

As I opened the King James' version of the Bible, it was obvious that the voice expected me to read it, which I did. To my bewilderment and amazement, the Bible opened on the Book of Luke, Chapter 11, and I started reading as follows:

And it came to pass, that, as he was praying in a certain place, when he ceased, one of his disciples said unto him, Lord, teach us to pray, as John also taught his disciples.

And he said unto them, When ye pray, say,

Our Father which art in heaven,
Hallowed be thy name.
Thy kingdom come,

Thy will be done, as in heaven, so in earth.
Give us day by day our daily bread.
And forgive us our sins;
for we also forgive every one that is
indebted to us.
And lead us not into temptation;
but deliver us from evil.

If you are reading this, and find it an amazing experience, can you imagine how I felt having gone through it?

I was so overjoyed and blown away at the experience, that after reading the prayer, I just lay back on the bed and said the words "thank you, thank you, thank you God." I must have repeated them about a dozen times, as I felt so blessed that the Lord would, once again, intervene and speak to me.

I don't have to tell you that I completely forgot that I had been contemplating doing the most atrocious thing any human being could do, besides killing another. The thought of suicide slipped out of my mind like water off a duck's back. It was as if I had experienced a moment of temporary insanity, because my whole being changed instantly.

"Realization is sudden. The fruit ripens slowly,

but falls suddenly and without return." ~Sri Nisargadatta Maharaj.

I must also point out here, that it took me some time to come to grips about writing this book and telling my story. I am baring my soul to you, telling you of my personal, private, and, what I regard to be, confidential information. I even thought writing about it might create some controversy but I was given the title of this book in meditation which implied it was time to share an aspect of my life's experience with you.

The important thing is that my story becomes a testimonial for those who have gone through, or are in the process of going through, similar experiences. My tale is meant to give moral support and strength.

It is peculiar that from childhood, especially after having had that encounter regarding the cross, I have always felt divinely protected. I have always felt that a higher Source watched over me and protected me and I have come to firmly believe that I am always in and sur-rounded by The Light.

I know my guardian angels are there, working over-time. But, in addition to them, I felt that there is a particular Being who resides in a different continuum, and who is available to me at all times. That being is generally referred to as God.

I want to give you an example of what I mean, as it became emphatically evident to me just before I became a teenager. From those youthful days I have always made requests to God by speaking, in private, the following words:

Dear Lord Jesus Christ, please guide me in the steps I take and the words I say day by day. Show me how to go and fill my soul with wisdom and love. Illumine my mind, light my pathway, and give me your hand to hold. I humbly ask thee to show me the work thou hast given me to do, that I may develop my soul and be of assistance and guidance to mankind.

By the time I got into my twenties, I had added the following words, which I say daily – as a part of my meditation:

Dear Christ in God, teach me to love, to be sustained by You, to be carried by Grace, fed by inspiration, led by guidance, and inspired by Divine Spirit. Thank you, Father God for hearing my prayer. Amen. OM.

TEN

The Guiding Force

Baring my soul to you and sharing many of my private experiences about my personal life - that I have shared with very few people - allow me to tell you of a few more extraordinary experiences I have encountered on my path. I will tell you about a few interesting incidents of the Spiritual or Divine guidance I have received on a number of occasions.

The first time - when I was at school in England and had this guidance - I was 19 years old, driving down the highway in my white Mini Cooper car in which were four of my friends. I was doing about 90 miles an hour when,

69

suddenly, a telepathic voice out of nowhere said to me, "Slow down, blowout!"

I was a bit startled, but took heed as I recognized the energy of that communication and lifted my foot off the gas pedal, then moved the car over to the left embankment, because everyone drives on the left in the United Kingdom.

Having moved over, I was in the process of stopping when my friends asked me what I was doing. I told them I was going to have a blowout so I needed to stop, and just at that moment the tire blew - and brought the car to a halt. They were baffled that I knew I was going to have a blowout, but as they did not know I was forewarned, they thought I was just psychic.

After graduating from the Royal Military Academy Sandhurst, I did an Arms Course in Hythe, England. On that course were many officers, mainly Captains and Majors from the US Special Forces. Those were the days of conscription in the US but these Officers were extremely professional and dedicated. Although the odd one was going to Vietnam for the first time, many of them were returning on their second and third tours of duty.

In the Officers' Mess where we dined and relaxed

in the ante-room, it was most interesting sharing each other's stories and having a few of the US Officers show us their 'battle scars' that seemed more like polka dots on their chests or backs made from exploding Claymore mines triggered by stepping on trip wires in Vietnam.

A fellow officer and I shared a flat in London, where we would spend our weekends and holidays. On the odd evening during the week, I would do the three-hour drive to London to attend a social function.

My return journey was always more challenging, as I had to decide whether to drive back the same night, or leave early the next morning since I had to get back in time for breakfast at 7:00 a.m.

One particular day, I left early afternoon, after classes, to attend another party in London. All went well, and I had a great time. I left shortly after midnight to get back in time to have a rest prior to breakfast.

Although I was physically, mentally, and spiritually fit, believe me, doing a three-hour drive when you are tired, partied out, and have a couple drinks in you is not the most exhilarating feeling – so please do not try it.

At twenty years of age, we can sometimes be very irresponsible, careless, and carefree. Sometimes we tend to think we are indestructible, and we bite off more than we can chew. About an hour after I started the return journey, I began to feel not only tired, but sleepy.

The incredible thing is that when I nodded off, I had horrible dreams which frightened me causing me to open my eyes, and increasing my adrenalin flow that kept me awake for a while longer, as I drove.

I exercised the utmost will power to stay awake, and I was only about an hour from my destination when I nodded off, once again, and tried to force myself to stay awake. Unfortunately, I really could not help myself and I fell asleep.

Suddenly I awoke, tightly gripping the steering wheel, while the car was heading off the road over the embankment. I don't know if you are familiar with the roads in England, in those days, and know that about a mile before a roundabout, there is normally a huge sign on the embankment that reads, "Slow down, roundabout ahead," or words to that effect.

Well, my dear friend, the car was heading straight for this huge sign, and I braced myself for the impact as I knew this was going to be my last breath on earth. All I had time to say was "God forgive me."

Then, suddenly, I felt a Force take hold of the steering wheel, at which time I released my tight control of it and allowed the Force to do whatever it desired. I had no choice as I had resigned myself to my fate, but for some strange reason I was kept alive.

This unknown Force turned my car in a complete 180 degree U- turn, steering it in the direction of the road and then turning left to line up the car on the left of the road pointing me in the direction of my onward journey.

Actually, as I am sharing this with you and putting it in writing for the first time, in reflection, I cannot remember whether I took my foot off the gas pedal or not, as everything happened so very fast.

When the Force lined up the car on the road, the car did not slow down, but as my hand was gently placed on the wheel, I could feel when the Force returned control of the car back to me from the free movement of the steering. I do not think I have to tell you that I was in a state of shock and every hair on my body stood up. My heart was pounding so loudly I could hear it, and I was virtually hyperventilating.

When I took control of the wheel, once again, all I said was "Thank you! Thank you so much for sparing my life. Thank you, thank you, thank you from the bottom of my heart."

Naturally, it was impossible for me to nod off again, and I was alert and wide- awake, for obvious reasons, the adrenalin flowed in excess. All I could think about was the incident and I was totally bewildered at a number of things. I wish to tabulate them, if you will forgive me.

Here are the things that I pondered:

1. It was an extraordinary miracle waking when I did in veering off the road.
2. In retrospect, it would have been impossible for me to execute a U-turn within the space allocated, and at the speed the car was traveling.
3. This amazing, intelligent Force was so attuned that it placed me back on the road in the direction I was traveling.
4. During the whole ordeal, the Force, the Energy said nothing whatsoever to me. No words were exchanged apart from my exuberant appreciation.

I must share my personal belief here. We are all protected by the Light of God. This gamut of protection includes our guardian angels, beings, aliens, family, deceased family members, and friends.

From my personal experience, I firmly believe they all reside in other dimensions of varying degrees. Jesus Christ said, *"In my Father's house are many mansions."* These worlds overshadow, and many are super-imposed on this dimension.

I have discovered that in order to create a link to those other dimensions we should:

1. Be conscious of the presence of the other dimensions and beings.
2. Give them permission to intercede in our lives where and when necessary
3. Give thanks for their ability and potential to protect us when called upon

Life is a very simple exercise. As mentioned in my previous book, life is a Divine play. This play will only last as long as your physical life does. It is imperative for you to choreograph your scenes well, and remember the play has certain rules and guidelines. If you harmonize and flow with them, you will be in harmony with all there is.

I have mentioned above a number of descriptive

choices of beings overshadowing us and I firmly believe all other intelligence are Light Beings. To make it simple, all matter is imbued with Intelligence, Consciousness, and Awareness manifesting and expressing as Energy, which is Light. The combination of all three is infused in every atom that comprises this Universe, including space and beyond.

The combination of this Trinity of Intelligence, Consciousness, and Awareness manifesting as Light/Energy is anywhere and everywhere in life, including our thoughts and words. This, to me, is God; which is a simplified way of referring to all that is.

My Guru gives a very nice analogy; he puts it this way. God, as Energy, is like gold and everything else conceived are just different ornaments of the same vein of gold. He also says that we are like fish and God is like water that flows around us, on top, below, and on every side of us and even through us as it does the fish.

ELEVEN

Contemplating The Lord's Prayer

When the revelation was made to me that night in bed about the Book of Luke, Chapter 11, relating to The Lord's Prayer, I went off to sleep with thanksgiving on my lips. I asked the Lord to give me the interpretation of the prayer, as it had to have a specific meaning for my despair, depression, and skewed mental and emotional state that night.

It took me weeks of contemplation and meditation to come to a real understanding of the prayer, which I will share with you in these final chapters. But first, I must tell you what I have learnt.

The Lord's Prayer is both a prayer and a meditation.

It is a prayer told in the form of a story that will lead those who say it to a state of being, beyond their wildest dreams, if it is said slowly with meaning and sincerity, and if we practice the true tenets of the prayer.

It is a meditation because the meaning of each word, each sentence, should be contemplated and then deliberated on to absorb the reality and impact of its meaning and effect. This exercise has the dynamics of creating change within each individual that is really inexplicable.

Members of the Christian clergy should and must stop rushing through such a sacred prayer during the service. I find this habit sacrilegious, an insult to the Lord who has given us a gift that we treat with scant regard.

I have yet to attend a church service anywhere that the priest, pastor, or evangelist says this prayer slowly with respect, love, meaning, and understanding. Perhaps, many of them do not know or understand the effects, affects, and dynamism of contemplation and meditation.

There is a lot of Power and Glory to be derived from such a beautiful prayer!

For those of you who have not discerned it, The Lord's Prayer has been given to mankind as a guide on how we may be infused with Cosmic Consciousness. To put it in simple layman's terms, this prayer is a sacred guide on how to be filled with the Holy Ghost or the Holy Spirit. You will notice that I have included Cosmic Consciousness, Holy Ghost and Holy Spirit in the same vein, as all three refer to a state of Illumination.

It is a very powerful prayer for the following reasons:

1. It guides us to recognize Our Source, the Creator.
2. The word **Our** Father refers to the collective, the kinship of Creation.
3. It eventually suppresses the ego.
4. It improves our health.
5. Provides healing for mental, spiritual, physical, and emotional issues.
6. It absolves sin and negates negative Karma.
7. It fosters guidance from Our Ultimate Source.
8. We become that on which we pray, contemplate, and meditate.

We have to graduate beyond the point of obsessing about the stories of the Old Testament and endeavor to view a deeper meaning in all biblical teachings of the New

Testament, as Jesus meant for it to be conveyed. We are mentally, spiritually, and scholastically beyond the stories of 2,000 years ago meant for those living in the past.

It is imperative to understand that Jesus Christ, or any other spiritual leader, did not share their wisdom for the point of teaching lessons to enhance a particular religion, but taught lessons for the world to benefit from their wisdom and teachings.

If they referred to a sect of religion it was not meant as a hard and fast rule, but as an attempt to share a deeper point peculiar to that religion and culture in which they were born.

TWELVE

Guidance from the Source

I have always been intrigued with the thought of doing the Lords will on earth as it is in heaven until I had a breakthrough in meditation.

Are you aware that when the Bible says, *"Ask, and it shall be given you; seek, and ye shall find; knock, and it shall be opened unto you,"* it is a literal statement? To be able to see this in action we must first have faith and believe that the spoken word is a very powerful energy and, therefore, must manifest. Try it and see for yourself! Remember that the thought, desire, and spoken word must be of the same intent.

The third verse of Chapter One in the Book of

Genesis reads: *"And God said, Let there be light: and there was light."* That is to illustrate to mankind how impacting are the spoken words.

More important, the Source could have given the illumination to instantly comprehend the correct interpretation of the prayer, but if I wanted to know more I had to work for it. Hence, the exercise in doing so caused me to both pray and meditate on each word, thereby showing me more emphatically how important, impacting, and revealing meditation is.

I also feel the other reason I was guided to this prayer is that it not only altered my decision to commit suicide, but took my mind off it completely. However, it took me months of meditation to fully understand the underlying depth and meaning of The Lord's Prayer.

Although this revelation was for my immediate benefit, I got the feeling that I was expected to share the deeper meaning with others. The thing is, the immediate revelation I was given at that specific moment, is the fact that there was no I or me, but **our**, implying that we are all **One Family of Light.**

As I lay in bed that night contemplating what I had just gone through, it was evident to me that the full meaning of the prayer would be revealed over time, which was by no means a surprise since I already knew that information flows freely from meditation. I also believed it was done in this way so that I could get the full impact of its meaning over a period before sharing it with others.

I have separated The Lord's Prayer into segments to assist readers in getting a better understanding of the meaning of the prayer.

Our Father which art in heaven,

This should illustrate to mankind that **God is One and all is One**, of the same family. He is the Source, Creator, God, Energy, Originator and is not only the Father of each of us, but the Creator of us all. We are all made from and in the image, that is of the same tree of existence and, therefore, in the same vein and of the same family. **One Family of Light!**

We just appear as different ornaments or reflections of the Creator. If you check on it scientists have already proven that this Universe is a dance of Light, pure Energy. To include the proof here would lengthen this book and the information is easily accessible in this information age.

God is the Energy in the entire Universe, behind the manifestation of the billions, trillions of stars, suns, planets, moons and heavenly bodies, and dimensions of all there is. Hence, God is the Energy behind the Trinity of **Creation, Manifestation** and **Dissolution** of everything there is.

As we pass on or die, our soul leaves the body and moves on. However, the body eventually decomposes; whether it is placed in a coffin or not, it still disintegrates at some time to replenish the earth - *"dust to dust, ashes to ashes."*

I strongly feel that our soul, that is Light, houses all our Intelligence, Karmic experiences, Consciousness, and the valuable intangible things learned on this plain; it qualifies which gate or house we enter on our passing, at dissolution or death - *"in my Father's house are many mansions."*

We should try to understand that the Creator of and in this dimension is nothing more than Light and pure Intelligence, although It is represented in the form of Jesus Christ.

In the King James' version, please take note of the word **which** are in heaven and not **who**, as this clearly is not referring to a person but to the vivifying power of Light.

Hallowed be thy name.

The name of God is *I Am*. Jesus said, *"I Am the way, the truth and the life."* In other words, what Jesus implied was I Am **is** the way, the truth and the **Light.**

As Jesus is God, it is a natural consequence to understand and believe that He is the Light. After all, Jesus Christ did make an absolute statement at the Crucifixion saying, *"The Father and I are One."* And if He is One with the Father then He is God.

The entire Universe and **All That Is**, is a manifestation from and of God and is logically His Kingdom, and, therefore, is His name. Any word that is made in reference to anything material or immaterial is a part of His Kingdom. It stands to reason that as everything is the name of God, then everything is holy or *Whole-ly.*

This is one of the aspects of understanding that differentiates a Spiritual person from a Religious person; the fact that the Spiritual person sees everything as an extension or expression of Creation, whereas the Religious person learns it from the dogma taught by clergy, not from his intuitive beliefs that come from the Source, God, who resides within each of us.

The word God does not denote a masculine God, but is used as a reference to the Creator, Light, or **All**

That Is. Since everything that God made is His Kingdom, or Home, then the meaning, I strongly feel, will eventually come to our realization. It is my belief that as Christians mature in the passage of time, religious perception, and understanding, they will mature in the understanding of Spiritual Philosophy and not in the dogma of Religion..

Thy kingdom come,

The understanding of His Kingdom or Domain, which is everywhere is already there and established in His Creation. The only place it is not understood or established is in the mind of man. Therefore, it is man's place to know and acquaint himself with the pantheistic or all inclusive nature of God.

Thy will be done,

When we are filled with ego and/or anger, we vibrate on a very low earthly frequency at which point it is difficult to intercept the higher octaves of Energy or Light. With low Energy it becomes impossible to tune into the more expanded state of consciousness and it is not easy to comprehend many things of depth simply because it is difficult to access. That is the reason why meditation is preceded with deep breathing and chanting or hymns, thereby raising the vibration or frequency of the body and mind to a feeling of holiness, purity, blessings, piety, and peace.

One of the purposes of increasing the frequency or vibration of the body is to also assist in subduing or overriding the ego, creating a sense of humility. It is also interesting to note that the ego cannot function efficiently in higher or subtle vibrations.

Here is a good description I once heard of the word EGO: *easing God out.* In a state of arrogance stimulated by the ego, it becomes virtually impossible to receive guidance from the Source. I previously mentioned that The Lord's Prayer is also a meditation which allows the practitioner to access the guidance and wisdom from that quantum level of very subtle vibrations from which all Divine Intelligence or guidance flows.

For those who do not understand the power or conduit of meditation, it is paramount to comparing the drive between a farm tractor and a Rolls Royce. The drive and style of meditation reaches higher speeds in effect and results and is vastly different, thus allowing an easier flow of the Universal guidance.

I find that prayer is usually a supplication to God or the Universe, whereas, meditation is opening oneself to the flow of God, the Universe, thus allowing us to be *programmed* or infused with God's will on earth.

Many do not view life as a single unit and, therefore, feel they are the doer, the pilot, not realizing that to think so is a reflection of the ego getting carried away. It is difficult for the ego to comprehend the intellect. Seeing plants and animals as different from us humans is an illusion of the ego.

As previously mentioned, the Energy encompassed in everything, or anything, in this world and the entire Universe, is what is called God in action. Nothing, absolutely nothing, happens without the expression of Energy. Therefore, the will of God is done in and through us with every breath.

As in Heaven, so in earth.

Heaven just happens to be another name for the Kingdom of God. Everything everywhere is heaven, including the other dimensions that exist. In heaven everything works in consort, in harmony, in tandem with the other. The only aspect of life that does not exist in such harmony and support is that of human beings.

Our very own perception and understanding of heaven and how this Energy flows to and through us, is very limited. If we were able to think in aesthetic terms and harmonize and flow with life, we would be in harmony with **All That Is.** Hence the reason why it is necessary to think in Light or to be filled with the Holy Ghost or Spirit. In modern terms it is called being filled with Cosmic Consciousness.

In my previous book *Expanding The Boundaries Of Self Beyond The Limit Of Traditional Thought*, I dedicated a chapter to the Steps to Transformation as it pertains to the expansion of Consciousness.

Give us day by day our daily bread

I have always been intrigued with this part of the prayer, as I believed that there was a much deeper meaning to this than the literal one of bread or food. We are told that if God could feed the birds and animals, and if He could array the Lilies of the field with such beauty, then think what He could do for us if we had Faith.

Therefore, the bread of God has to be the intangible tenets that would make us better and more noble human beings by realizing our Divinity as co-creators of His, since we are made in His image and likeness. For clarity I will list but a few of those intangible tenets that we may wish to ask for as our daily bread:

They are love, wisdom, truth, intelligence, knowledge, understanding, intuition, peace, faith, patience, beauty, joy, health, happiness, zeal, imagination, eternal youth, tolerance, prosperity, opulence, bounty, purity, will, power, strength, success, among other Spiritual gifts that you may add to this list.

I can imagine that there are many readers who do not believe in, or have thought about reincarnation and I know this will be a challenge for you to overcome.

And forgive us our sins; for we also forgive every one that is indebted to us.

Now whether we are believers or not, I would think many, if not all, of us would like to have our misdemeanors, transgressions or sins against others absolved or forgiven. Many atheists and agnostics I have met, believe in being forgiven for some indiscretion they committed and, in return, they wish to forgive because even they like harmony as we all do.

Forgiving and being forgiven is not necessarily a religious act but, indeed, an act of civility and self preservation, particularly health-wise as it is a terrific psychological feeling to believe we have our indiscretions forgiven by those we have transgressed.

The heading of this section allows us to let go of our egos and reflect on everyone and everything, including ourselves as we have held grudges, hurt, anger, negative memories, thoughts and actions against many people in our lives.

To harbor revenge or hold on to not forgiving another is to cause resentment which triggers the body to start commencing the reproduction of cancer cells which feeds on negative energy and thought. I feel very strongly that resentment fuels sickness particularly cancer. Actually, to not forgive or be resentful is to live in the past, which is certainly not healthy, so it means releasing evil or negative thoughts and replacing it with forgiveness and love.

Not to forgive ourself or another person, regardless of who it may be, is like infesting ourself with organ-eating worms and hoping it will satisfy our hunger for revenge.

Whether it be mother, father, sister, brother, uncle, aunt, cousin, friend, boss, co-worker, stranger, it is imperative to release the pain being held for the situation or the person. It becomes necessary to put your faith into action and let go and let the Creator, the Source, the Lord, God, the Light take care of the situation.

I cannot begin to explain to you, as somehow words

do not adequately describe the feeling of freedom, ease, satisfaction, joy, and peace that is felt in being the divine soul that you are when you take that one step to forgive. It gives you a terrific sense of achievement, of accomplishment in doing so.

"The weak can never forgive. Forgiveness is the attribute of the strong." ~Mahatma Gandhi

Not practicing forgiveness also ages you by accentuating or causing many wrinkles to appear on your face, in addition to causing all sorts of afflictions and ailments.

Harboring resentment or a grudge obscures the brilliance and color of the Aura and most importantly, it becomes virtually impossible to live in the present, in the moment of Now. So not forgiving is to live in the past!

Learning to live in the Now is the common denominator to living a life of eternal joy and happiness.

This can only be achieved when there is a vacant space created in the mind, so that enlightenment and inspiration may enter in its place.

"Enlightenment cannot be attained, nor forced. It can only happen...It can appear only when it is given a vacant space to appear in" ~Sri Nisargadatta Maharaj

Again, I strongly feel that harboring resentment is

one of the major reasons that causes many of the negative experiences to which we are subjected, bearing in mind that we reap what we sow.

I am aware that many Christians do not believe in reincarnation because it is not taught in the religion, but I do know many Spiritual people, whether they be Christians, Jews, Muslims, Hindus, Buddhists, or otherwise, who believe in reincarnation.

However, whether one believes in reincarnation or not, we are all the sum total of our past experience. We each have in our Cosmic composition or DNA, a Cosmic Vibratory Frequency, as I refer to it, that has recorded within us an account of every experience, whether negative or positive, that we have had from the beginning of existence - normally referred to as the Akashic Record.

This includes transgressions by us and against us in every lifetime. It is all based upon this Karmic principle of cause and effect, that we must account for those past actions by reaping the benefits, good or bad, negative or positive, of that which we have sown in our current and past lives.

Therefore, in asking for our sins, transgressions or negative Karma to be forgiven, the Lord forgives us by

Divine or Cosmic Grace. Remember that forgiveness applies not only to this life but to all our previous and parallel lives as well.

And lead us not into temptation; but deliver us from evil.

Our egos have become so inflated, and we have become so arrogant, that we have the audacity to believe that we are actually the doer of things. We have not come to terms with the fact that the Energy, God or Light is the intelligent creative vivifying power that energizes us and the Universe into action.

So here we ask the Lord, the Source, to keep us on the path of Light and not allow us, in our arrogance or ignorance, to steer from that path; for to do so, we land into temptation of believing we are the doer.

In the same way we get absolved of our past Karma by the sheer asking of the Lord, is the same way that we are absolved of and kept from temptation and delivered from evil or negativity through the power of Grace.

The word sin is a verb that describes a feeling - it derives from Latin, to feel guilty. Karma on the other hand, is basically action and inaction, sowing and reaping, cause and effect. There are three types of Karma: actions from past lives, actions from present life, and actions that will have to be accounted for sometime in the future.

This is why The Lord's Prayer should be a daily meditation as we accumulate negative Karma daily. The good Karma we don't have to worry about as it can only manifest in good, bringing joy and happiness; but each day, the negative should be cleansed.

THIRTEEN

All is One

The Christian saying that Jesus shed his blood to save us from our sins is very difficult to comprehend. To my understanding, Jesus went through the challenges of His Ministry so He could, as well as other teachings, give us the key to eternal life through an understanding of The Lord's Prayer, if we prayed and meditated upon it. That exercise would absolve us from all past sins or negative Karma and free us to experience our divinity.

The amazing thing about prayer, meditation, philosophy, religion, spirituality, and ontology, is that nothing can be proven to others. Spiritual occurrences can only be proven through one's personal experience.

I remember, as a teenager, observing people, particularly those who attended church, and there were very few of them that I could fairly say reflected an Aura and a pattern of behavior that was an incentive for me to glorify God.

This is the reason why we should not stereotype people and judge anyone on appearances as we do not know the purity and intent of their heart.

Knowing God, our Source, is a personal experience!

We are all on a holy path with our Source. Each person has a different earthly mission resulting from their Karma, experience, upbringing, sense of appreciation, and the value they place on life. Could this be the reason why Jesus said, *"Judge not, that ye be not judged."*

I had an earnest desire when I was about 11-years-old to find this wrathful God I heard about. My intuition, belief, and faith would only allow me to believe in a wonderful loving power, certainly not that negative concept.

I realized that there was much too much confusion about the concept and reality of our Creator. There were just too many persons I knew and heard about who feared God like I had feared the *boogey man* as a child. This could just not be right; somebody was duping us with an incorrect interpretation.

To satisfy this desire, the Bible was the only Holy Book I had access to as a child. When I decided to read the New Testament for clarification and understanding, I asked the Lord to give me the wisdom to discern His teachings.

In addition, I actually put myself in the place of Jesus and wondered, *OK, if I am the Lord, what is it that I am trying to tell the mass of people who have little or no education, and how can I do so in simple language, giving them good analogies that they can understand?*

As a child, I had always known I was blessed as the Creator, God, sent me to this dimension for a specific reason. My main purpose was to learn as much as I could about Our Source while negating my negative Karma. It is from that sense of desire that I was gifted with the ability to discern, as I opened my mind to being receptive to intuitive direction, allowing me to be blessed with the understanding and wisdom I have shared with you.

Another thing I discovered is that if The Lord's Prayer is said at least 15 times continuously in the morning, before commencing daily activities, the prayer becomes an excellent meditation and the day would be filled with very pleasant or miraculous surprises.

However, to observe the miracles one has to be very aware and look out for them. So many wonderful things happen to people daily, no matter how small, but the bewilderment of such occurrences are missed simply because peoples' minds are preoccupied and are not attuned to their surroundings. This is why it becomes necessary to learn how to still the mind and focus on the present.

You may wish to try this prayer and meditation yourself, as I have discovered that it does make me feel as if I am walking on Cloud Nine - or some other cloud.

Remember, an amazing reality with this prayer is that it is a story, a guide for mankind to arrive at a stage of Cosmic Consciousness or to be filled with the Holy Ghost or Spirit, which is Light.

For the time being, this is the end of my testimony; the rest will be left, hopefully for another book. I am very pleased the Lord, our Source, has allowed me the privilege of sharing this with you.

It is imperative for you to understand that not everyone will share or have the same experience as I did, as it is directly proportionate to the desire and quality time spent in prayer and meditation.

Should you feel the urge to commit suicide, please do not wait for a mystical experience to intervene and save you, but instead phone a hotline where there are professionals who always volunteer their time to help others.

No one is an island unto themselves, and we all need someone to talk to. It is also important to understand that God may, in His discretion, communicate through any medium whether it be someone else, an animal, bird, plant, or incident. The secret is being aware of God's presence at all times, whichever way you may view the Source.

In summary, no matter how difficult the path gets, as the Oral Roberts Ministries once said, *"Expect a miracle!"*

One Love, Love All, All is One, Love is One!

Poem of Enlightenment

- The Circle of Consciousness

Consciousness is Life

Life is Nature

Nature is Creation

Creation is Universal Intelligence.

Universal Intelligence is Divine Will

Divine Will is Creative Energy

Creative Energy is Atomic Energy

Atomic Energy is Light.

Light is God

God is Awareness

Awareness is Consciousness

Consciousness is Divine Will.

Divine Will is Creation

Creation is Nature

Nature is Life

Life is Consciousness.

Taken from the Book -
Expanding The Boundaries Of Self
Beyond The Limit Of Traditional Thought.
ISBN: 9780976498804 by Oliver H Jobson © 2004

101

If you live outside the USA and are in need
of help or guidance please consult a doctor,
member of the clergy or the National Suicide
Prevention Lifeline in your country.

National Suicide Prevention Lifeline

Need help? In the U.S., call 1-800-273-8255

National Suicide Prevention Lifeline
www.suicidepreventionlifeline.org/

"No matter what problems you are dealing with, we
want to help you find a reason to keep living.
By calling 1-800-273-TALK (8255)
you'll be connected to a skilled, trained counselor
at a crisis center in your area, anytime 24/7."

Suicide.org - Suicide Prevention, Awareness, and Support.